This STEM Book
was purchased through the
Didi Barrett Funds
for Arlington Libraries
2016

Careers in Construction

Engineer

WITHDRAWN

Kristi Lew

Cavendish
Square

New York

Published in 2016 by Cavendish Square Publishing, LLC
243 5th Avenue, Suite 136, New York, NY 10016

Website: cavendishsq.com

This publication represents the opinions and views of the author based on his or her personal
experience, knowledge, and research. The information in this book serves as a general guide only.
The author and publisher have used their best efforts in preparing this book and disclaim liability
rising directly or indirectly from the use and application of this book.

CPSIA Compliance Information: Batch #CW16CSQ

All websites were available and accurate when this book was sent to press.

Cataloging-in-Publication Data

Lew, Kristi.
Engineer / by Kristi Lew.
p. cm. — (Careers in construction)
Includes index.
ISBN 978-1-5026-0976-2 (hardcover) ISBN 978-1-5026-0977-9 (ebook)
1. Engineering — Vocational guidance — Juvenile literature.
2. Civil engineering — Juvenile literature. I. Lew, Kristi. II. Title.
TA157.L49 2016
620'.0023—d23

Editorial Director: David McNamara
Editors: Andrew Coddington and Kelly Spence
Copy Editor: Rebecca Rohan
Art Director: Jeffrey Talbot
Designer: Alan Sliwinski
Senior Production Manager: Jennifer Ryder-Talbot
Production Editor: Renni Johnson
Photo Research: J8 Media

The photographs in this book are used by permission and through the courtesy of: Hero images/
Hero Images/Getty Images, cover; VanHart/Shutterstock.com, 4; Andrew Zarivny/Shutterstock.
com, 7; imageshunter/Shutterstock.com, 12; © Robert Harding Picture Library Ltd/Alamy Stock
Photo, 17; maigi/Shutterstock.com, 22; Ed Jones/AFP/Getty Images, 28; auremar/Shutterstock.com,
34; © dpa picture alliance/Alamy Stock Photo, 38; Luciano Mortula, 40; Goodluz/Shutterstock.
com, 43; AP Photo/Northwest Herald, Lauren M. Anderson, 47; Chip Somodevilla/Getty Images,
52; Goodluz/Shutterstock.com, 56; THOMAS KIENZLE/AFP/Getty Images, 58; Rawpixel/
Shutterstock.com, 60; Goodluz/Shutterstock.com, 65; wavebreakmedia/Shutterstock.com, 68;
Monkey Business Images/Shutterstock.com, 71; Tim Roberts Photography/Shutterstock.com, 77;
bikeriderlondon/Shutterstock.com, 79; zhu difeng/Shutterstock.com, 82; zimmytws/Shutterstock.
com, 88; Kathryn Scott Osler/The Denver Post via Getty Images, 91; NakoPhotography/
Shutterstock.com, 96; NASA/NASA Goddard Space Flight Center/File:NASA's BARREL Mission
Launches 20 Balloons.jpg/Wikimedia Commons, 101; Naufal MQ/Shutterstock.com, 103.

Printed in the United States of America

Table of Contents

Engineers designed the 605-foot (184.4 meter) Seattle Space Needle to withstand winds traveling up to 200 miles per hour (321.9 kilometers per hour) and earthquakes measuring more than 6.8 on the Richter scale.

Introduction

Any structural landmark you can think of—the Empire State Building, the Hoover Dam, or the Golden Gate Bridge—is the direct result of the hardworking, dedicated men and women employed in the construction field. Complex building projects such as these require the cooperation of many conscientious and skilled workers, including **architects**, electricians, plumbers, carpenters, and many others. Integral to this team is the work of civil engineers.

Engineers are dreamers, **innovators**, creators, and inventors. They are also professional problem solvers. They use their knowledge of science and mathematics, as well as their creative thinking skills, to design and build machines, circuits, electronics, medical devices, spacecraft, and structures. Through innovation and application, engineers provide solutions to problems that face society.

The field of engineering encompasses a wide range of specialties and activities. Some of the major branches of engineering include aerospace, manufacturing, nuclear, materials, biological, mechanical, electrical, chemical, and civil. Civil engineers focus on the built environment, which includes all the basic physical and organizational facilities that allow society to function. They are responsible for the world's tallest buildings, the interstate highway system, and the success of the moon landing. They design and oversee the construction of homes, theaters, sports stadiums, hospitals, bridges, oil rigs, airports, and space satellites.

The field of civil engineering can be broken down even further. Some of the major subspecialties of civil engineering include architectural, construction, structural, environmental, geotechnical, and transportation. However, other branches of engineering may also be involved in some capacity in the construction field. Mechanical engineers, for example, may work on the elevators and other mechanical components of a high-rise building, while electrical engineers tackle its electrical systems. Materials engineers study metals, ceramics, polymers, and composites to determine how each material can be improved and used to its fullest potential. Their knowledge is then applied to choose the materials best suited for a construction project.

The 726-foot (221 m) tall Hoover Dam and the 1,905-foot (581 m) bridge that bypasses it are both marvels of modern engineering.

Engineers in the construction field can work on new projects, such as buildings, bridges, or dams. Or, they can use their problem-solving skills to determine how best to repair or maintain an existing **infrastructure**. Infrastructure refers to the basic physical structures and organizational facilities needed for a city, state, or country to function. These structures and facilities include roads, railroads, airports, wastewater treatment plants, canals, power and water supply facilities, and others.

No matter what the project is, engineers are responsible for making sure their designs are functional, **aesthetically** pleasing, and safe. Before the first brick is laid, they must understand the stress of a load, or **forces**—such as wind pressure, the strain created by a potential earthquake, or the traffic burden—that may be applied to a structure. To do this, construction engineers must assess the strength of building materials and weigh their suitability against their cost, financially and environmentally. Today more than ever, engineers must consider the needs of the environment by using green materials and building practices. These highly trained professionals must use their technical skills and their knowledge of physics and chemistry to determine what will work—and what will not—before millions of dollars are spent or **natural resources** are wasted.

Most engineers who work in construction focus on one particular sector. They might, for example, specialize in the construction of residential or commercial buildings. Or they may focus on some aspect of the nation's transportation system, which includes highways, bridges, airports, and harbors. Alternately, an engineer may spend their career providing clean water to people by designing and maintaining wastewater treatment plants, reservoirs, dams, and the related infrastructure that moves water to and from homes, businesses, and institutions. Other specialty engineers might concentrate on the design, management, and installation of heating, ventilation, and air-conditioning systems. The possibilities are endless.

Civil engineering is one of the few technical professions where the results of an individual's efforts are truly visible. People who work in this field have the opportunity to change the face of the nation. They establish and maintain the connections required to produce power and wealth, change the built landscape and, in the process, have an opportunity to better every citizen's standard of living. They protect public health, welfare, and safety by ensuring people have access to clean water and air, safe and sound housing, and modern transportation. Engineers also play a key role in the development and maintenance of docks, harbors, airports, railways, and reliable roads that connect one nation to another. Without these vital links, international trade between nations would be much more difficult, and the US economy would suffer.

In the coming years, the United States is going to be in desperate need of trained engineers. According to the National Science Foundation, 5.5 million science and engineering degrees were awarded in 2010. Nearly a quarter of those degrees (24 percent) were granted in China. Seventeen percent were earned by engineers and scientists in the European Union. Only 10 percent of the worldwide engineering and science degrees were awarded to American students. That gap grows even larger if only engineering degrees are taken into account. In 2010, 31 percent of bachelor's degrees in engineering went to newly minted engineers in China; only 5 percent went to Americans. The demand for highly trained engineers with cutting-edge technical skills and world-class leadership abilities is only going to grow as the United States faces an aging infrastructure and the ever-changing needs of a twenty-first-century society.

With the proper planning and education, you can become one of these individuals. The education you need begins in high school. Start by taking as many science and math classes as possible. Join your school's science and engineering clubs, and participate in competitions such as the Conrad Spirit of Innovation Challenge, the FIRST **Technology** Challenge, or the Tests of Engineering Aptitude, Mathematics, and Science (TEAMS) challenge. Good grades and participation in extracurricular activities can help you get into a top engineering school. Working with a team of like-minded individuals to design and build innovative projects is a lot of fun, too!

The Great Wall of China is made up of many different sections. If all the sections are measured, the wall is 13,670 miles (22,000 kilometers) long.

CHAPTER 1

Civil Engineering Leaders

Today's engineers use complex mathematics and high-speed computers to bring their visions to life. Because of the high-tech tools used in this field, many people think of engineering as a profession that sprang up during the Industrial Revolution, or even later. However, the construction industry, and the engineering skills used within it, dates back to the early days of civilization, when humans began building shelters for themselves. People in ancient times not only built homes, they also constructed monuments, palaces, roads, dams, bridges, canals, harbors, tunnels, lighthouses, and sewage systems. The engineers who designed these structures may not have had any formal training, nor were they called engineers. Yet, they still applied the concepts of engineering to their projects.

Two thousand years ago, Roman engineer Vitruvius wrote that buildings should be three things: strong, aesthetically pleasing, and useful. From the Pantheon in Rome to the Brooklyn Bridge in New York City, engineers have demonstrated that those objectives are still not only desirable but also essential to any structure. The ancients designed and constructed an amazing array of aqueducts, bridges, tunnels, and buildings, especially given the tools and techniques they had available to them. The invention and refinement of materials such as cement, cast iron, and steel allowed engineers to tunnel farther underground and build higher into the sky than ever before. The trailblazers in the field of civil engineering provide a glimpse at the breadth of experience and the types of projects that civil engineers have been involved with in the past, and the ones that they dream of constructing in the future.

Engineering in Ancient Times

One of the most influential architects, engineers, and construction managers that has ever lived built his masterpiece nearly five thousand years ago in Egypt. This master builder's name was Imhotep. With simple mathematics, few tools, and no machinery, he designed and supervised the construction of the Step Pyramid.

Standing 206 feet (62 m) high, at that time, the Step Pyramid was the highest structure ever built. Imhotep is considered a visionary because he was the first known person to have used stone as a building material. Before that time, structures had been made out of compressed mud, shaped into bricks. Stone was much stronger than these bricks and allowed the Step Pyramid to be built larger than any structure ever before. The design of this early pyramid was a stepping-stone toward the later construction of the Great Pyramid of Giza.

Some of the earliest engineers were actually military engineers. The Great Wall of China, which was originally conceived around 200 BCE, is considered by many to have been the first large-scale engineering project. The high walls and fortifications of the Great Wall were designed to protect China from potential invaders. Beginning in the eighth century BCE, the military engineers of ancient Rome designed and built catapults, towers, and other fortifications that were developed for the protection of land, goods, and people. Bands of Roman soldiers traveled with proto-civil engineers who helped build roads and bridges as the armies advanced.

When military engineers were not concerned with battle, they turned their attention to civil projects, such as aqueducts, bridges, canals, and dams. The word "civil" is related to the word "citizen." It means of, or relating to, ordinary citizens and their concerns, which differentiates these projects from military or religious affairs. The techniques used to create these ancient engineering projects formed the basis of civil engineering today.

The Industrial Revolution

During the eighteenth and early nineteenth centuries, the Industrial Revolution ushered in many new manufacturing processes that led to the creation of new building materials. These materials, such as iron and metal **alloys**, quickly changed the world's landscape. New manufacturing techniques created strong materials, such as cast iron, from which structures could be built. Cast iron is an iron-carbon alloy, which is a mixture of metals or the mixture of a metal and another element, such as carbon or silicon. Alloys have particularly desirable properties, which are different from those of the pure metal. Cast iron was desirable as a building material because, compared to pure iron, it was relatively inexpensive, durable, and easily shaped. The first metal bridge, which spans 102 feet (31 m) across the Severn River in Shropshire, England, was made of cast iron and opened in 1781. Another iron-carbon alloy commonly used in the construction field is steel. The difference between cast iron and steel is the percentage of carbon found in the alloy. Brass and bronze are alloys, too. Brass is an alloy of copper and zinc and bronze is a mixture of copper and tin.

The first person to call himself a civil engineer was an Englishman named John Smeaton (1724–1792). He used the term to distinguish himself from the military engineers of the day. During his lifetime, Smeaton designed and constructed thirty-five major civil engineering projects. He is most famous for his design of the third Eddystone Lighthouse, which

The current Eddystone Lighthouse was completed in 1882. Its design incorporated several of Smeaton's techniques, including dovetailing and the use of marine cement.

marked a major breakthrough in how lighthouses were built. Smeaton's design was constructed entirely of stone. He joined the stones together using a technique called **dovetailing**, which provided the lighthouse with a strong base that could withstand the pounding of the waves. The fourth, and current, Eddystone Lighthouse was constructed using many of Smeaton's techniques. In addition to the lighthouse, Smeaton was also responsible for the Forth and Clyde Canal, a 35-mile (56 km) waterway that spans central Scotland. He also designed the Perth Bridge, which opened in 1771 and continues to carry automotive and pedestrian traffic to this day. In 1771, Smeaton founded the first professional engineering organization. It was originally called the Society of Civil Engineers, but it was renamed the Smeatonian Society of Civil Engineers after his death.

Building an Empire

The chief engineer of the Erie Canal system, Benjamin Wright (1770–1842), has commonly been called the "father of American civil engineering." The Erie Canal is a 363-mile (584 km) canal, requiring eighty-three **locks,** that runs through New York State from Albany to Buffalo. Construction on the canal, which created a passable channel from the Atlantic Ocean to the Great

Lakes, began in 1817. This gigantic feat was accomplished using nothing but horses, mules, wagons, wheelbarrows, and hand tools, plus an awful lot of work from thousands of dedicated laborers. When the passage was completed in 1827, it was the longest canal in the world. Today, it is part of the New York State Canal System.

A young, self-taught engineer named Canvass White (1790–1834) worked under the supervision of Wright. Canvass White was sent to England to study the canal systems. While there, he observed the use of a limestone mix to waterproof the canal locks. Upon his return, he developed a hydraulic cement, which is cement that will harden underwater, using local limestone found near the Erie Canal. White's ingenuity effectively made him the first concrete engineer in the United States.

Another influential engineer who lived and worked during this era is Stephen Harriman Long (1784–1864). Long was not just an engineer, but an explorer and pioneer as well. During his career, Long built railroads, bridges, forts, and dams. He ventured into the unexplored American West, charting the land as he went. Long's maps would later prove invaluable for the westward expansion of the United States. Long was the first American engineer to use mathematical calculations to analyze bridge **trusses**. He invented the "X," or

"Long truss," in 1830, and went on to patent designs for **bracing** and counterbracing bridges. He also developed formulation tables that would help later engineers determine the proper curve radiuses and optimal grading for railroads.

Long's formulation tables went a long way in helping one of the greatest engineering projects of the mid-nineteenth century come to life—the world's first transcontinental railroad. Designed and executed by Theodore Judah (1826–1863), the Pacific Railroad would link America's east and west coasts. Its completion in 1869 transformed the country's economy and advanced its development. Judah, who previously worked on the Erie Canal project, was also instrumental in securing the necessary funding that allowed the Pacific Railroad to be built. He would not, however, live to see the completion of his project. He died of yellow fever in 1863. He was thirty-seven years old.

In the early 1900s, engineers were hard at work on new technologies. Every day, the knowledge they gained, the discoveries they made, and the inventions they created grew more sophisticated. Up to this time, wood, brick, and stone were the most commonly used building materials. In 1885, that all changed with the construction of the 180-foot (54.9 m) Home Insurance

Building in Chicago, Illinois. The Home Insurance Building, designed by William Jenney (1832–1907), was one of the first structures to be built with a metal frame. Using steel instead of the more traditional stone or brick drastically reduced the weight of the building's **structural members**. This in turn allowed the building to be constructed much higher than it could have been using **masonry** techniques, without the fear of it buckling under its own weight. For this reason, Jenney is known as the father of the modern skyscraper.

In the early 1900s, the United States government began to build a national network of interstate highways. However, it was well after the end of World War II that the Interstate Highway System was officially authorized with the Federal Aid Highway Act of 1956. According to the Federal Highway Administration, as of May 2015, the system is 46,876 miles (75,440 km) long. The only country with a larger highway system than the United States is China. Not only were countless workers involved in the construction of the Interstate Highway System but, once underway, the highways allowed for much easier access to the suburbs. This, in turn, led to a huge housing boom that employed many others in the construction field.

THE WORLD'S FIRST FERRIS WHEEL

Not all engineering marvels are bridges, roads, and skyscrapers. Some are just downright fun. Officials overseeing the World's Fair held in Chicago in 1893 wanted to build something that would showcase American ingenuity. They were also desperate

The London Eye is a modern version of the traditional Ferris wheel. Unlike Ferris's invention, the Eye is supported on only one side, which allows the structure to hang over the River Thames.

to outshine the iron lattice tower, called the Eiffel Tower, which had been unveiled at the last World's Fair in 1889 in Paris, France. American civil engineer George Washington Ferris (1859–1896) rose to the challenge. He designed and built a

twenty-five-story-high rotating wheel that, when fully loaded, could carry over two thousand passengers in thirty carriages. Each glass-enclosed carriage was about the size of a railroad car. The wheel measured 250 feet (76.2 m) across and was made up of more than one hundred thousand parts, including an 89,320-pound (40,515-kilogram) axle. It towered above Chicago's tallest building at that time. Ferris's wheel made one complete revolution every ten minutes and treated people from around the world to a breathtaking aerial view. The original wheel was demolished in 1906, ten years after Ferris died of typhoid fever at the age of thirty-seven.

A national network of roads is an impressive endeavor, but another amazing engineering feat carried out during the twentieth century was the first manned space mission to the moon. The moon landing occurred on July 20, 1969, and was a tremendous success thanks to the work of more than four hundred thousand engineers, scientists, and technicians. One of the engineers who was instrumental to the mission was John C. Houbolt (1919–2014). Houbolt earned his civil engineering degree from the University of Illinois. He was the visionary behind the idea of sending a single launch vehicle, consisting of a mother ship and a landing craft, to the moon. Some people thought Houbolt's idea was too complicated and dangerous, but he did not give up. Eventually, he convinced NASA to try out his smaller, lighter spacecraft. After his contribution to the space program, Houbolt did not just sit back and retire. He went on to study the force of wind shear and air turbulence on high-speed aircraft wings and invent a way to reduce flutter. This discovery led directly to the development of stealth fighter jets and modern bombers.

Modern Construction

Engineers work with scientists, architects, and other professionals to invent and improve modern building methods and materials. The tallest building in the world today is the Burj Khalifa in Dubai. At 2,300 feet (700 m), the building took five years to complete. The invention of super-strong steel, high-speed elevators, and powerful water pumps were necessary to make skyscrapers like the Burj Khalifa possible. Skyscrapers' frames are often constructed of steel, making them strong so they can withstand outside forces, such as wind pressure. High-speed elevators allow people to travel up and down a tower in a reasonable amount of time, and powerful water pumps are needed to carry running water to the top of a building.

In engineering, there is always the dream of building bigger and higher. Engineers are still trying to figure out what techniques and materials they could use to bring renowned architect Frank Lloyd Wright's vision of a mile-high (1.6 km) building to life. Wright sketched the idea in 1956. One day, perhaps, engineers will invent the materials and methods needed to fulfill Wright's vision.

New Technologies

With the development of software programs, such as **computer-aided design (CAD)** and computer-aided manufacture (CAM), the field of civil engineering changed yet again. These powerful programs allow engineers to design, create, and test simulations of nearly any type of structure under countless scenarios. Three-dimensional (3-D) design and modeling software saves time, money, and labor, greatly increasing efficiency.

Engineers and architects have been using CAD programs since the 1960s. At first, the software was very expensive and limited to use in government offices and by a handful of large companies. In time, however, the software became more economical, and more architectural and engineering firms invested in it. By the 1980s, CAD had become a widely used tool.

Nearly all of today's architects and engineers use CAD programs on the job. Realistic renderings allow them to visualize a design before construction begins. Simulations can be run to show how a building will withstand the forces associated with hurricanes or earthquakes. The strength and appropriateness of construction materials can also be tested. If a design does not work, the architect or engineer can easily tweak the style or change the materials that will be used before any money is spent. Once a design is finalized, the program can also be used to make a list of parts and materials needed, as well as organize other details that save time.

CAD is not only used in the design of bridges, buildings, and highway systems. It is also used to design theme park attractions. Engineers use these programs to dream up and design rides and other attractions. New amusement park rides should be fun and thrilling but, above all, they must be safe. Rides may incorporate power systems that include compressed air, electric motors, or magnets. New designs often have computer-controlled safety features to keep people in their seats. Engineers are needed to design, review, and oversee the construction of all these components.

Architects and engineers use CAD-created models and **blueprints** to communicate their ideas to others. Clients, inspectors, and other professionals can review the blueprints and give feedback or suggestions to make the design better.

Engineers today are also concerned with developing green, or environmentally conscious, building designs. They might, for example, design a ventilation system that allows hot air to rise naturally throughout a building. Not only does this design require less energy to pump hot air out of the building, but it has the added benefit of heating the upper floors, too. Engineers have designed some buildings, such as the German parliament building, to use mirrors to reflect sunlight into the interior of the building. The sunlight is used to heat the building. The mirrors also direct light downward, so less electricity is needed to light the building.

A 3-D model can help engineers, investors, and the general public visualize a project before construction begins.

Today's engineers are involved in construction projects that would have sounded like science fiction just a few decades ago. Hong Kong's International Airport, for example, was built by creating artificial land in an area between two Pacific islands that was once filled with water. Along with this innovative airport, engineers have also built mega spaceports, the world's largest radio telescope, ten-story underground buildings, and many other radical construction projects.

Along with Frank Lloyd Wright's mile-high building, engineers hope to one day tackle another extreme project—a bridge over the Bering Strait. The Bering Strait is a waterway that connects the Pacific Ocean with the Arctic Ocean between Russia and Alaska. The proposed bridge would stretch 55 miles (90 km) across the strait and require more than two hundred massive piers, weighing more than 55,000 tons (50,000 metric tons) each. The design concept includes roadways that would carry automobile traffic as well as high-speed trains. It also incorporates a pipeline running beneath the road that could carry oil from Asia to the United States. To bring this idea into being, engineers visualize each pier being specially shaped to deflect any icebergs that float near the bridge. These piers would need to be made of a material that can withstand prolonged periods of extreme cold, as well as pressure from the ice.

Women in Construction

Historically, both construction and engineering have been male-dominated fields. Women have faced barriers in training and advancement. However, as the years go by, this is changing.

Ellen Swallow Richards (1842–1911) was a pioneer for women in science. In 1870, she became the first woman to be admitted to the Massachusetts Institute of Technology (MIT). Three years later, she received a chemistry degree from MIT, as well as a master's degree from Vassar College. Her thesis explored the chemical composition of iron ore. In 1876, Richards successfully convinced MIT that it would be worthwhile to open a laboratory focusing on the work of female scientists. Seven years later, after MIT started awarding undergraduate degrees to women on a regular basis, the Women's Laboratory at MIT was closed.

Ellen Richards also established the first sanitary engineering course at MIT. At the time, sanitary engineering was mainly concerned with methods that could improve public heath and safety by efficiently disposing of wastewater and delivering clean drinking water. As an instructor of sanitary engineering, Richards taught some of the first environmental engineers. She also produced the world's first water purity tables in 1877.

Richards made many significant contributions to the health and safety of American citizens over the course of her career. One of these achievements was the identification of "sick building syndrome." This syndrome can cause serious chronic illnesses, such as headaches and respiratory problems, in people who work in affected buildings. Richards determined that insufficient ventilation was often to blame for the worker's poor health conditions.

Following in Richards's footsteps was Elizabeth Bragg Cumming (1859–1929), the first woman to earn a bachelor's degree in civil engineering. Although Cumming received her engineering degree in 1876, there are no records indicating that she ever worked in the profession.

Unlike Cumming, another outstanding female engineer, Emily Warren Roebling (1843–1903), did not have a college degree. However, she certainly practiced the profession. Roebling learned about engineering principles through her own observations and experience. Her father-in-law, John Roebling (1806–1869), designed the Brooklyn Bridge, which spans New York's East River and joins Manhattan to Brooklyn. In 1869, before construction got underway, John Roebling was killed in an accident while surveying the site. Emily and her husband, Washington Roebling (1837–1926), stepped in and completed the final design details. The pair planned to oversee the construction of John Roebling's dream. Shortly after construction began, however, Washington, who designed and worked in the watertight structures used to construct the parts of the bridge that were underwater, developed decompression sickness, or "the bends." Rendered paralyzed, partially blind, and deaf in the accident, Washington was often unable to speak. Emily began overseeing the day-to-day details of the bridge's construction. Carrying information to and from her husband's sickbed, Emily quickly became well versed in civil engineering. By the end of the project, she was answering all the questions, as well as solving problems for workers and public officials. Nearly everyone involved treated Emily as the chief engineer on the project, and she is credited for the bridge's timely completion.

The women who worked in construction in the 1970s and early 1980s also helped forge a career path for many women in the following generations. Today, female engineers are not as rare as they used to be. In fact, according to the Society of Women Engineers, in the 1980s, only about 5.8 percent of all engineers were women. By 2012, that number had risen to 14 percent.

Women still lag behind men in numbers, but the women who work in the construction field today find that more and more people are supportive and accepting of them. While not all barriers have been overcome, society has made tremendous progress in educating and advancing the careers of women in both construction and engineering. Today, there are numerous schools, organizations, and resources that focus on helping women build successful careers in the construction industry.

Women currently working in the engineering field have some good advice for young women thinking of pursuing this career: First, be confident and understand your motivation for wanting the job. People may challenge your career choice, but if you meet their challenges head on and believe in yourself, you will have access to an exciting and rewarding profession. Second, you may have to prove yourself, especially in the beginning. You can do this by not asking for preferential treatment. Be willing to cover construction operations in bad weather or lead the night shift. Stand out in the rain if you must, even if you could easily be sitting inside a nice heated field office instead. In short, be tough and show that you take your job seriously. Work hard and be concerned about the quality of the finished construction project. Once you show that you know what you are doing, and prove that you are willing to work hard, people will give you the respect you deserve.

Many engineering and construction firms, and most public sector offices, too, actively seek out women and minorities to create a more diverse workforce. Schools and organizations also offer scholarships to women pursuing scientific, technical, engineering, or mathematics (**STEM**) degrees.

Civil engineers often collaborate and work in teams on design projects.

CHAPTER 2

Education and Training

What makes a good civil engineer? Many of the people working in this exciting and rewarding field share a few things in common. Most of them have been interested in the way things are built from an early age. They are fascinated with the ways in which homes, bridges, skyscrapers, and other structures transform an empty landscape. One of their favorite questions is "what if" and they enjoy solving problems—all sorts of problems. They are interested in math and science, they are curious, and they have an interest in helping people live life to the fullest. If any of these traits sound familiar to you, you may be suited to a career in engineering and, more specifically, an engineering career in the field of construction.

What It Takes

Successful engineers need to have a wide range of skills. When most people think of engineering, the first set of skills that comes to mind are technical and analytical thinking skills. An engineer working in construction needs to be up to speed on current construction methods and technologies. They use the principles of calculus, trigonometry, and other advanced mathematics in order to analyze, design, and troubleshoot a project. They must be ready to interpret contracts and technical drawings, plan a project strategy, handle unexpected issues and delays, and solve any problems that come up. The best way to start improving your technical skills now is to make sure you develop a solid background in science and mathematics, including algebra, geometry, trigonometry, and calculus.

While engineers certainly must have solid technical skills to draw on, they also need to be creative and curious. Every day, engineers face challenges that test and stretch their problem-solving skills. They are constantly coming up with new ideas or ways of doing things, as well as thinking of ways to improve existing ones. As teenagers, many engineers enjoy taking things apart to learn how they work. Future civil engineers often look at existing structures and think of ways they might improve the design. They may also join clubs and organizations, such as the For Inspiration and Recognition of Science and Technology (FIRST) LEGO League. They often compete in contests and competitions like the FIRST Robotics or Technical Challenge, or the American Society of Civil Engineers (ASCE) National Concrete Canoe Competition. These organizations and team events give you the hands-on experience of designing and building while learning and applying real-world engineering techniques. This type of innovative thinking, or thinking "outside the box," will help prepare you for a profession in which every day you are called on to solve problems.

Most people who enter the engineering profession have a passion for problem solving. They enjoy designing and conducting experiments, and they have an enthusiastic interest in lifelong learning. Budding civil engineers think about how people interact with structures in their surroundings. They ponder the ways in which good infrastructure can improve life and how bad infrastructure can have a negative impact on someone's standard of living. They tend to have an interest in how to build infrastructure that can sustain and protect the environment, while also maintain the health and safety of society. Above all else, they are insatiably curious. They are always wondering why things are the way they are.

Students design, build, and test their concrete canoes as part of the International Concrete Canoe Competition, sponsored jointly by the ASCE and the American Concrete Institute (ACI).

It takes time to design a structure and to make sure it will be functional and safe. The engineers that worked on the Golden Gate Bridge spent more than sixty-five years developing the design before building ever began. For this reason, engineers in the construction field must be patient, but they also need to be persistent. Sometimes an engineer's original idea does not work out and they must start all over again. The problem still needs to be solved, so they do not give up. They just keep trying new ideas and testing possible solutions until they find one that will work.

Life as an engineer can be exciting, but challenging. Things don't always go to plan on a construction project. A construction engineer needs to be able to handle unanticipated obstacles and work with design changes efficiently and effectively. To do this, they must be flexible and have the ability to see these obstacles as opportunities instead of problems. Engineers must be confident enough in themselves and their skills to realize that with hard work, research, and determination, the problem will get solved.

Civil engineers have to take their jobs very seriously. They check and double check their calculations. They also have others check their calculations. They must be able to accept constructive criticism and suggestions from others without becoming defensive or feeling insulted. They must remember that there could be lives on the line. One error in an engineer's force calculations on a bridge or skyscraper design can result in extremely unsafe conditions.

Most civil engineers, especially those working on larger projects, work as part of a team. As their career progresses, an engineer may find themselves leading a team, too. Lead engineers must have good decision-making and leadership skills. They will need to choose laborers and subcontractors, determine how best to

The Dubai skyline emphasizes skyscraper design elements, such as varying diameters and multi-faceted surfaces, which help counteract the effects of wind pressure.

deal with problems, and effectively delegate tasks to construction workers, lower-level managers, and others. They will need to make these decisions quickly to stay on time and within budget. These engineers are often working on complex projects with many parts. They cannot be easily distracted.

Often, an engineer needs to balance opposing priorities, such as the detailed design of a structure and the feasibility of getting the project done to meet its budget and safety regulations. They must have the ability to monitor and evaluate the work being done on a construction site, and they must be willing to listen to the people working with and for them. While a lead engineer is ultimately responsible for a project, they cannot be everywhere at all times. They must be open to listening to issues and suggestions from the team they have assembled. They must not, however, be easily swayed without solid evidence that changes need to be made. One way to learn how to become a better team player now, and to develop your leadership skills, is by joining a team sport. Try to gradually work your way up into a leadership role, such as a team captain.

Lead engineers on large projects and self-employed construction engineers must also show **initiative**. They have to be self-starters. Lead engineers will work with a variety of people with different personalities and skills. They must be dedicated to making sure the team they have assembled stays on task and works well together. Any conflicts must be dealt with effectively to prevent problems within the team. Self-employed engineers must be energetic and proactive in finding new clients and generating their own business opportunities. They must market their skills and be willing to learn new ones that will make them more marketable. They must be able to bid on projects and work independently, but also be able to work as part of a team. In other words, they have to be adaptable.

Another key set of skills an engineer needs are communication skills. Field engineers may need to explain to a specialist exactly what a problem is and why the specialist's expertise is being sought. The specialist may not be able to come to the site, so the field engineer must clearly explain the problem. Once they receive the specialist's report, they will need to communicate these results to the client and explain the solution to their workers. Lead engineers are in constant contact with clients, inspectors, and construction crews. They must communicate work plans clearly and explain work stoppages when they occur. Problems and setbacks need to be accounted for. An engineer may also interact with the public, especially if they are working on a larger public works project. Public works projects are funded by local, state, and federal governments and may include building a new hospital or repairing worn-out roads. As such, engineers need excellent public speaking skills. These skills allow them to give clear orders, explain complex information, and discuss technical details with inspectors, architects, and other construction specialists.

Engineers need to have excellent verbal and written communication skills. They must often explain complex, technical information in person as well as in writing.

Clear, well-thought-out speaking skills are critical but so are writing skills, specifically technical writing. Engineers write proposals, plans, and budgets. They need to document progress and slowdowns for clients and others involved in the project. They must be able to communicate with other professionals, such as building architects, landscape architects, and urban and regional planners, verbally as well as in writing. Engineers in charge of projects give presentations when bidding for jobs as well as status updates throughout the project.

Junior engineers often help prepare presentations as well. If you can, take some public speaking and writing courses at your school or through your local community college. These classes can help you build strong presentation and communication skills. You can also build strong communication skills by asking questions and sharing your ideas in class. Ask for advice or help when you need it from teachers, mentors, tutors, or classmates. Brainstorm solutions to problems, all sorts of problems, with many different people.

Engineers also address budget matters, coordinate and supervise workers, choose staff, and establish good working relationships with colleagues and employees. To do so, they need strong business, organizational, and time management skills. They must plan the various stages of construction that need to take place for any given project. For example, an engineer needs to be aware that they cannot schedule the framing to go up before the **foundation** is laid. They need to be able to meet deadlines since one phase of construction often relies on another and setbacks can delay the entire project.

Today's engineers also rely on their computer skills. Some of these skills are technical, such as the ability to understand and use CAD programs. Others are more basic, such as touch-typing. Most engineers do not have administrative assistants and are expected to prepare reports and memos. Nearly everyone in construction management today has a computer on his or her desk. In addition to CAD programs, many construction engineers will use cost-estimating and planning software to determine how much material is needed for a project and how best to transport it to the jobsite. A community college is a great place to learn and advance your computer skills.

Along with honing your abilities by taking extra science, math, writing, public speaking, and computer courses, experience in the construction field, in any capacity, is an added bonus. Working for a construction company during school breaks or volunteering for organizations such as Habitat for Humanity can help get you into a competitive engineering program, not to mention an entry-level job.

The world is changing faster than ever. You must be prepared to keep learning. It also helps to have a genuine thirst for knowledge, a need to know how the world works and why. Be curious and resilient—and, above all, learn from your successes as well as your mistakes. All engineers do.

Education

It was not until the mid-nineteenth century that civil engineering was first named as a separate educational discipline. In 1819, Norwich University, a private military college in Vermont, established the first civil engineering class, solidifying the difference between architecture, military engineering, and civil engineering. In 1835, Rensselaer Polytechnic Institute became the first school to award a civil engineering degree.

Once the first civil engineering course had been developed, societies were not far behind. The American Society of Civil Engineers (ASCE) was founded in 1852. Similar societies sprang up around the world. Since then, the number of colleges and universities around the world that offer degrees in civil engineering has continued to increase.

There was a time when people who worked in construction could move up through the ranks based solely on experience. Today, this is rare. Supervisors, managers, and engineers are relying more on sophisticated computer software to do their jobs. Construction materials and methods change rapidly and more people are taking advantage of educational opportunities. They are working toward college degrees and going back to school to get advanced degrees. This surge of educated

Engaging in engineering challenges can help build problem-solving skills. These students successfully completed their challenge by designing a structure made out of paper that could support the weight of a book.

applicants creates enormous job competition. To get a job in construction engineering today, you will almost certainly need some education beyond high school. This may include a four-year university degree, a two-year program at a community college, or a certificate program at a technical school.

The best way to prepare for college-level work is to enroll in a college preparatory curriculum in high school. Courses should include physics, chemistry, higher-level mathematics, public speaking, writing, and computer courses. Joining after-school programs that focus on debate, science, engineering, and team-building skills help as well.

Post-Secondary Education

Bachelor's degree programs in engineering usually devote the first two years of study to mathematics, basic science, humanities, social sciences, and introductory engineering courses. The last two to three years are spent studying courses related to a specific kind of engineering. In general, course work usually includes classes such as analytical geometry, linear algebra, and statistics; physics and chemistry; engineering mechanics and systems; and fluid dynamics.

Civil engineers who choose to specialize in heavy construction, which includes the building of highways, bridges, airports, and wastewater treatment plants, also study geology and soil mechanics since these projects often involve a lot of excavation and underground work. Engineers planning to focus on the management and construction of electrical systems will take many of the same courses on circuits that are required for electrical engineering. However, they also take courses to learn about the construction side of the business, too.

Engineers specializing in construction engineering take a mixture of courses that include basic science, engineering, and technology. They also study business management. Specific courses in contract management, construction methods, people management, project estimating, and construction cost and scheduling control are all needed. All civil engineers take basic courses in structural analysis and design, geotechnical engineering, transportation engineering, steel and concrete structures, foundations, circuits, statics, construction safety, and heavy construction equipment, methods, and materials. Depending on the specialty, more advanced courses may be called for in any of these disciplines.

Most university programs in civil engineering combine engineering design, business management, and courses that focus on sustainability. Courses such as these teach budding engineers how to successfully balance the technical aspects of engineering with the practical application of construction. Most programs also include a mixture of classroom learning, laboratory research, and hands-on experience at a construction site.

Licensing

Before an engineer can serve as the lead on a project, he or she is required to pass a licensing exam administered

ENGINEERING CO-OP PROGRAMS AND INTERNSHIPS

Some engineering programs require students to complete an internship or a cooperative education program, commonly called a co-op, before they graduate. Both of these programs provide students with the opportunity to gain real world, hands-on job experience. Today, this is something most employers expect to see on a résumé. The main difference between the two programs is that students participating in a co-op generally stop taking classes and work full-time while they are in the program. Co-ops are paid positions and last anywhere from three to twelve months. An internship, on the other hand, may be paid or unpaid, and is often completed during the summer. Some interns choose to work part-time during the school year so they can still take classes. The experience provided by internships and co-ops is invaluable.

Some employers expect new engineers to have one thousand to three thousand hours of work experience before they graduate. For this reason, the earlier a prospective engineer starts interning or lands a co-op, the better. A college student who starts working in their sophomore year can gain more on-the-job training than someone who starts as a senior. They can also work for different companies, which is an excellent way to develop a professional network and to figure out exactly what type of engineering you enjoy the most. According to the 2015 Internship and Co-op Survey conducted by the National Association of Colleges and Employers, 51.7 percent of interns and co-op students accept a full-time position in one of the companies they worked with before graduation.

by an accredited certification board. In general, there are four steps to becoming a licensed and registered professional engineer. The first involves gaining some knowledge of the engineering profession, whether through post-secondary education or hands-on learning. This is followed by completing the Fundamentals in Engineering/Engineer-in-Training exam (FE/EIT), gaining on-the-job professional experience, and passing the professional engineer (PE) exam. However, requirements vary from state to state. The best way to find out what is required in your state is to contact local organizations, such as the state engineering society, and ask.

Writing the FE/EIT exam does not require a completed college degree. In fact, engineering students usually take the test their senior year before they graduate, immediately following the completion of their related coursework. In some states, you are not even required to be enrolled in an engineering program to take the test.

The FE/EIT is known by different names in different states. However, it is a standardized test and, therefore, covers the same material and is structured the same way regardless of where it's written. The six-hour, multiple-choice exam covers 110 questions and is prepared and graded by the National Council of Examiners for Engineering and Surveying (NCEES). Practice tests,

Engineering students engage in various projects to help hone their computer and problem-solving skills. Designing solutions to multiple problems also helps to ingrain engineering principles.

with example problems and solutions, are available from the NCEES website (NCEES.org).

Most entry-level engineering jobs require applicants to take and pass the FE/EIT exam. However, an engineer is still not licensed after passing the exam. To become licensed, an engineer must take and pass the PE exam. In many states, an engineer is not eligible to take the PE exam until he or she has completed at least four years of on-the-job training. However, requirements for this test also vary from state to state. It is best to research the necessary qualifications in your own state before applying for the exam.

Like the FE/EIT, the PE exam is a standardized, national exam. Its formal name is the Principles and Practice of Engineering, but most people just call it the PE exam or the professional engineer exam. It is an eight-hour exam that is split between a morning and an afternoon session. Like the FE/EIT, this exam is prepared and graded by the NCEES. More information, including the specific topics covered by different specialties, can be found on their website.

Civil engineers specializing in structural engineering have their own exam, called the SE. The SE is a sixteen-hour exam that is spread over two days. It tests the engineer's ability to safely design buildings or bridges.

The practice of requiring engineers who offer services to the public to meet specific criteria in order to call themselves "engineers" began in 1907. The FE/EIT, PE, and SE tests have been developed to protect the public. Practicing engineers who have passed the FE/EIT, but have not yet passed the PE exam, must work under a licensed engineer if they are working on a public works project. Only licensed PEs may take the lead on these projects.

Most of the time, lead engineers on public works projects have postgraduate degrees in civil engineering. According to the US Bureau of Labor Statistics (BLS), more than one in five civil engineers hold a master's or a doctorate degree. To advance into a management position, a postgraduate degree, a professional engineer's license, and extensive work experience are often needed. That being the case, pursuing an advanced degree can provide the possibility for greater opportunities, more responsibility, and higher earning potential as an engineer.

Engineering Technician

If you are interested in engineering work but you are not sure you are ready to attend a four-year college program, you may want to pursue a job as an engineering technician. Engineering technicians assist senior engineers in their work. Most employers today prefer engineering technicians to have at least a two-year associate's degree from an accredited community college. A certificate or diploma from a technical or vocational school, or equivalent on-the-job experience, may be acceptable as well. Students in a four-year engineering program may work part-time or during school breaks as engineering technicians, too.

An engineering technician's job description is nearly as varied as that of an engineer. A typical day may include reading and reviewing blueprints, preparing preliminary cost estimates, or researching current building codes.

Technicians often accompany a licensed civil engineer to the construction site. They may then come back to the office and help draw up a design in a CAD program. They may conduct experiments while testing soil samples or concrete in a laboratory. They may set up and monitor equipment or conduct a review of the work being done to make sure everything stays on schedule and on budget. Engineering technicians document project activities and data which they use to prepare reports for the lead engineer, keeping him or her up-to-date on the various parts of the project. Engineering technicians cannot approve designs or supervise overall projects, however. Only licensed engineers are certified to perform these job duties.

Part of being an engineering technician includes helping civil engineers avoid problems that waste time, effort, and money. Therefore, it is important to have critical-thinking skills. Technicians must have strong decision-making skills that allow them to quickly assess what information is most important and which actions are needed to keep a project running smoothly. Technicians also need good observation skills. They must be able to identify problems on the jobsite and report back to their supervisor. Technical skills are equally important. An engineering technician must be able to understand the reports, plans, and technical drawings that are approved and

Cost Estimator

Another related technician job is that of cost estimator. Cost estimators gather all the data that influences the cost of a construction or remodeling project. This data usually includes the cost of materials and labor, the price of utilities, insurance, tools, and various other things that make up the total cost of a large project. Cost estimators need to take into account whether utilities, like electricity and water, are easily available

A cost estimator works with clients, architects, engineers, and other professionals to develop a reasonable budget for a project.

at the site or if crews will need to come in and dig trenches to lay new lines. They have to assess whether there will be any special challenges, such as the need to blast through bedrock to excavate a basement. Cost estimators examine the technical drawings prepared by an architect or an engineer to see what types of materials are needed. If the design requires facing a building with granite instead of brick, for example, the cost estimator will take into account the added expense of the material and the additional labor costs associated with granite. A cost estimator's work can help determine if a job will be profitable and whether it should be undertaken at all.

A successful cost estimator must pay close attention to detail. They must also have a willingness to recheck their calculations, sometimes several times. The ability to handle stress as the requirements of a job change and their work needs to be redone is also helpful. Cost estimators use algebra, geometry, trigonometry, and sometimes calculus in their work. Their jobs require them to be able to read blueprints, construction specifications, and other technical documents. They need strong computer skills and the ability to learn new software programs quickly. Some cost estimators get their jobs after years of experience in construction but, as with other jobs today, more and more companies are seeking people who have studied construction, engineering, or architecture to do this job.

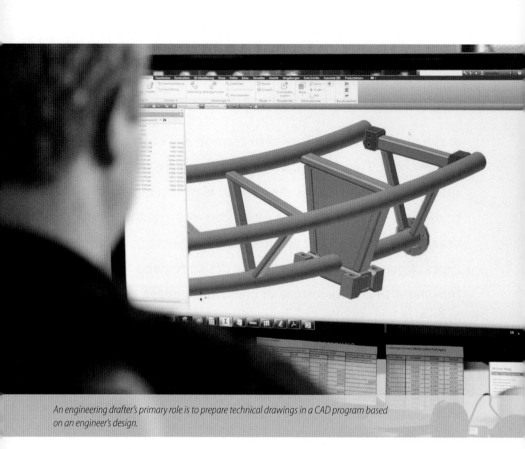

An engineering drafter's primary role is to prepare technical drawings in a CAD program based on an engineer's design.

passed down by the lead engineer. They should also be able to write well-organized, clearly written, detailed reports to communicate the day-to-day activities on a jobsite.

Like an engineer, an engineering technician relies heavily on science and mathematics to do his or her job. Therefore, helpful high school classes include courses such as chemistry, physics, calculus, and computing. All technicians must be computer-literate and math-savvy. They must be able to learn how to operate equipment quickly and communicate clearly, both verbally and in written form.

Certification may not be necessary to enter the field as an engineering technician; however, it can be helpful for advancement. The National Institute for Certification in Engineering Technologies (NICET) certifies engineering technicians. Certification involves passing an exam and providing documentation of work history, references, and verification of specific experience from a supervisor. Every few years, recertification is required. Recertification is necessary to update skills, improve knowledge, and continue professional development. The time between recertification dates depends on where an engineering technician works.

Another possible career path is to become a drafter. A drafter is a technician who specializes in the preparation of technical drawings. Engineering drafters work under the direction of a licensed engineer or architect. An architect or engineer might come up with the rough draft of a design using CAD software. They may then turn the design over to a drafter to fine-tune and complete.

Both engineering technicians and lead engineers work with cost estimators to come up with a budget for the project, project managers who keep everything on schedule, and specialty contractors who are responsible for different aspects of the project. It does not matter what type of project it is—building anything is a team effort.

An engineering design team collaborates to finalize the plans for a project.

CHAPTER 3

On the Job

To complete their projects, civil engineers must work with a variety of people. They may collaborate with technicians, surveyors, cost estimators, and specialized engineers to design, construct, and maintain various types of infrastructure. Not all civil engineers build structures, however. Some of them use their knowledge of math and science to design and build new equipment, study and perfect new materials, and investigate and validate new processes that other engineers can use in their work. No matter what type of projects they work on, civil engineers generally do so for the benefit of society.

Types of Civil Engineers

Civil engineering can be subdivided into many different specialties, several of which have considerable overlap.

Some of the subspecialties of civil engineering include architectural engineering, structural engineering, and construction engineering.

Architectural Engineers

Architectural engineers apply engineering principles to the design and planning of buildings. Their focus is on the structural integrity of the building and the efficiency of the building's systems. They are responsible for the design of the heating, ventilation, air-conditioning, plumbing, electrical, and fire protection systems, as well as the building's **acoustic** and lighting plans. Architectural engineers take courses in mechanical, electrical, and structural engineering as well as architectural and design classes. Architectural engineers are most likely to work on residential and small commercial projects, such as houses, stores, and small businesses.

Structural Engineers

Structural engineers are mainly concerned with the strength and loading of a structure. Many structural engineers work as consultants to architects and general contractors. An architect or contractor will design the structure and the structural engineer will analyze the design and calculate the loads that might be placed on the structure. Loads might include the weight of snow or ice, or the forces exerted by winds or an earthquake. The structural engineer is responsible for making sure the appropriate materials, such as steel, concrete, masonry, or wood, and structural systems, such as beams and columns, are chosen. This work is essential to ensure that a structure is strong enough to withstand its expected loads.

To make a structure strong, structural engineers must understand the forces that hold buildings up as well as the forces that are trying to bring a structure down. The key to success is a solid understanding of basic physics as well as having extensive knowledge of available construction materials and the ways in which they work together. A structural engineer knows that some shapes are naturally stronger than others. A square, for example, is a relatively weak shape. If you were to nail four pieces of wood into a square, then apply pressure to one of the sides, the square easily turns into a diamond. Triangles, on the other hand, are much stronger. Three pieces of wood joined to make a triangle form a rigid structure and will not twist out of shape. This is why many bridge supports and roof trusses incorporate triangles into their design.

In the case of a bridge, a structural engineer needs to understand several forces that will act on the structure. They must calculate the weight the design must hold without buckling, the amount of traffic it needs to support, and what kind of temperatures and weather the materials need to withstand. Other stresses, such as the shaking that occurs during an earthquake or the twisting that could be encountered during a tornado may also need to be accounted for. All of these factors must be determined and analyzed before the shape and style of the bridge, and the number of supports that might be needed, can be figured out.

Construction Engineers

There is a specialty profession in civil engineering specifically called a construction engineer. A construction engineer combines the design aspects of a project with construction management. These engineers are not only responsible for creating the design and preparing blueprints for a project, but also with the day-to-day scheduling and supervision on the jobsite. They assess the quality of construction, enforce all safety rules, and monitor the performance of subcontractors. They also apply for permits needed from local, state, and federal agencies. They are responsible for making sure that a project complies with building and environmental regulations. If a project does not meet these expectations, they may also need to apply for and justify special permission, or make changes to the project to meet the regulations.

Construction engineers design and oversee construction projects. They spend most of their time on the jobsite.

Construction engineers often consult with other specialty engineers, such as geotechnical and environmental engineers. A geotechnical engineer studies the rocks and soil that support civil engineering projects. They apply their knowledge of soil science, materials, mechanics (the behavior of structures when subjected to forces), and hydraulics (the properties of liquids or fluids) to design foundations, retaining walls, and other necessary structures. They often study survey data and topographical maps to make sure that the area proposed for a project is stable enough to support it. Environmental engineers determine the environmental consequences of a proposed project. They are often consulted to make sure a project complies with government regulations. They may also analyze and address any environmental problems and provide a risk assessment for the project.

Like most other engineers, construction engineers use CAD software to prepare blueprints. This software helps the engineer to calculate important figures and easily create the design. Once the blueprints have been drawn up, the engineer prepares a presentation outlining deadlines, cost estimates, materials required, and other important details. Then, the clients are consulted. Any changes that are needed must be made before the project can move forward. This may take several rounds of refinement until all parties are satisfied with the design and safety of the project, as well as how much it will cost to build.

During the building phase, construction engineers spend much of their time on the construction site. They work with a project supervisor to make sure schedules are met. They also make sure that safety measures are being followed and that subcontractors are properly licensed and have the appropriate experience to do the job. He or she will also inspect any work to make sure it meets with the approved plans. If problems are found in the design or in the construction, the construction engineer is responsible for finding solutions to fix them. They are also usually responsible for the design and construction of temporary structures, such as the field office, that will be used during construction. Construction engineers may work for small contracting companies, government agencies, or large construction firms.

Other Types of Engineers and Professions

In places susceptible to earthquakes, an earthquake engineer is likely to be involved in the design phase of any large structure, especially those that serve the public realm. Earthquake engineers are concerned with the design of structures that can withstand the forces of an earthquake. They may study the possible consequences of earthquakes on a specific structure, as well as consult on the best way to construct and maintain structures to meet with earthquake building codes. Earthquake engineering is usually thought of as a subdiscipline of structural engineering.

Other professionals who contribute to the infrastructure that civil engineers oversee include the men and women who specialize in materials science and engineering. Materials science is the study of the basic characteristics of materials, such as concrete, asphalt, strong metals like steel and aluminum, and polymers like acrylic and carbon fiber. Materials engineering also focuses on the protection and prevention of **corrosion**, a possible source of material failure. A materials engineer

THE ENGINEERING DESIGN PROCESS

All engineers follow a specific, step-by-step method to create their designs and form their ideas. The first step in the engineering design process is to identify a problem that needs to be solved. Once identified, an engineer will attempt to learn as much as possible about this problem. They ask themselves things like: Why does this problem exist? Why does it need to be solved? If this problem is solved, what would be the best outcome? They then begin to gather information about the

Brainstorming as many solutions as possible is an important step in the engineering design process.

problem by doing research, talking to others, and asking lots of questions to better understand the problem.

The second step in the engineering process is to brainstorm many possible solutions. At this stage, an engineer tries not to throw away any ideas, no matter how expensive, silly, or impractical they seem. Often, engineers will work in groups to come up with as many ideas as possible to solve the problem. Once they have exhausted their creativity, the individual or the group will determine which of these possible solutions is the most economical and feasible.

Engineers then create a plan and make a model of the solution. This step is most often done on a computer with CAD software. Using the software, engineers can also test their ideas by running simulations of specific conditions, such as an earthquake or a hurricane. They use the test results to improve and refine their design. This testing and improvement step is often repeated several times until the group is satisfied that they have the best possible solution.

The final step in the engineering design process is to communicate, or share, the design with others, including the client. Feedback is given and, once again, the testing and refinement process may be repeated until all parties are completely satisfied. Only then does construction begin.

may study and develop paints and finishes to coat a material to prevent corrosion, or they may develop alloys that are able to stand up to the elements.

A Day in the Life of a Civil Engineer

Civil engineers do not usually build the structures they design. Instead, construction crews use their technical drawings to build the structure to the engineer's specifications. So, what do civil engineers do all day? Well, that largely depends on their specialty. Architectural engineers, for example, will likely spend most of their day in an office drawing and refining designs on the computer. A construction engineer, on the other hand, will spend the majority of their day at the construction site, often in the construction field office itself. Other civil engineers will spend different amounts of time between their office and a jobsite. At one time or another, however, just about all civil engineers will visit the construction site to make sure everything is being built correctly and to answer any questions.

A typical engineer spends some of his or her time planning what needs to be accomplished each day. Doing this may require reviewing scheduled appointments and making preparations for any meetings they may have to attend. They will probably also spend some time working

Most engineers juggle multiple projects and have numerous responsibilities. They take advantage of tools that can help them do their jobs as efficiently as possible.

on a new design or the revisions of an existing one, reading and responding to e-mails, and fielding phone calls.

Unless they are self-employed contractors, most engineers work in an office with their coworkers and team members. One or several people may be responsible for talking to local government officials to determine what public works projects are in discussion. It is important for a civil engineering firm to know what projects are in progress and what the public opinion of those projects might be. It is also important that they know what projects might be coming up. This can help the firm plan for, and bid on, future projects.

Most engineers spend a lot of time on the computer, either designing, running simulations, or troubleshooting. They use CAD software to design a structure that will meet the requirements laid out by the client, while keeping in mind any **constraints**. A requirement dictates the features that the structure should have or functions that it must do. A parking garage that must hold a certain number of cars of a certain size, for example, is a requirement. A constraint is a limit placed on a design. For example, the size of the lot a parking garage is to be built on may limit its size. An engineer must balance all of these factors to come up with the best solution.

A typical engineer juggles several projects at once, all of which may be in different stages of the construction process. Gary Searer, a structural engineer for Wiss, Janey, Elstner Associates in Burbank, California, for example, told reporter Greg Aragon in an interview with *California Construction* that he is often "trying to get one report out the door and start a new project at the same time."

An engineer may spend part of the day inspecting some aspect of a current project at the construction site. This involves making sure that all the work being done meets building code requirements and suggesting potential improvements to the current design. Building codes are updated frequently. Some engineers report that the bulk of the requests they get for an on-site job deal with ensuring these codes are being met.

The Northbrook, Illinois, office of Wiss, Janey, Elstner Associates also does forensic analyses on engineering failures. Engineers in the company have worked on several projects that have had marked significant moments in our nation's history. These projects include examining some of the New York City buildings affected by the September 11 terrorist attack, the Interstate 35W bridge collapse in Minnesota, and the Interstate 5 tunnel fire in California. Searer says he loves his job because it requires "creativity to solve the problems and diligence to figure out why something happened." Understanding what happened and why these structures failed helps future engineers avoid design flaws and prevent loss of life.

Structural engineers may be called in after a disaster strikes. If an explosion has occurred, for example, a structural engineer will be called to determine how best to stabilize the building so that it is safe for forensic experts or inspectors to investigate. After the investigation is complete, the structural engineer may also work with the company that owns the building to determine how best to fix any structural damage that has occurred. They may also be called in after a hurricane or an earthquake has damaged a building.

The Collapse and Rebuilding of the World Trade Center

On September 11, 2001, the two 110-story-tall Twin Towers, the centerpieces of the World Trade Center complex in lower Manhattan, collapsed after being struck by two passenger airplanes. In the spring of 2002, the United States Congress charged the National Institute of Standards and Technology (NIST) to conduct an investigation into the disaster. Civil engineer S. Shyam Sunder was named the lead investigator. Sunder and the engineers on his team modeled the aircraft impact and the resulting fires and verified their findings with photographic evidence, laboratory tests, and videos of the actual collapse.

Sunder's team concluded that a combination of events led to the structural failure of the steel frames that held up the Twin Towers. First, the sprinkler systems in the buildings were nonfunctional due to damage resulting from the impact of the aircraft. In addition, multiple fires, fed by jet fuel, erupted on the floors above and below the impact zones. Although the jet fuel burned up fairly quickly, the contents of the buildings—the workstations, computers, papers, and carpeting—kept the fires going. The initial high temperatures and the duration of the fires weakened the steel structure of the buildings.

This made the steel pliable. As the fires continued to burn, the steel supports that attached the floors to the external walls of the building began to sag, pulling the external columns inward. This inward bowing, which was captured in photographs, was what ultimately led to the collapse of both buildings.

The National September 11 Memorial now sits on the site in remembrance to the three thousand people who lost their lives on that day. The centerpieces of the memorial, two reflecting pools that each cover nearly an acre (.4 hectares) of land and feature 30-foot (9.1 m) manmade waterfalls, were built within the footprints of the original Twin Towers. They are the largest manmade falls in North America. The 110,000 square foot (10.22 square meter) National September 11 Memorial Museum lies seven stories below. One World Trade Center, which is also called the Ground Zero Supertower or the Freedom Tower, reaches 104 stories and 1,776 feet (541 m) into the air, making it the tallest skyscraper in the Western Hemisphere. A testament to the strength of the American public and to the hard work of the engineers, architects, and more than one thousand construction workers involved in the project, One World Trade Center opened for business on November 3, 2014.

Structural engineers may be involved in the design of new buildings and the restoration of historical ones, too. For example, they might study a reservoir with leaking sections to try to figure out how to fix it, or they may work with problems within a mass transit system. In each case, their job is to determine whether or not the structure is safe, what is causing the problem, and figure out how best to solve it.

On any given day, engineers working on public works projects may also meet with local officials to discuss a proposed project for the city. They would discuss the requirements of the project and possibly visit the future construction site to determine a preliminary cost estimate. Then they would return to the office where they might sketch up a rough drawing and start researching costs. Some of the costs that might be associated with such a project would be the price of the land, survey costs, identifying any hazards that might need to be removed, and how plumbing and electrical lines would be run. They would also need to budget in materials, equipment, and labor costs.

Engineers working in large and small firms may have to attend staff meetings in order to review ongoing projects to make sure they are progressing on time and within budget. As a team, they may also discuss new

Complex highway interchanges require time, money, and the hard work of many individuals to efficiently design and build.

products, materials, or processes that could save time or money on future projects. Any new material or method must be inspected and approved before it can be used on any public works project. The team must decide who will test and inspect which items so that they may be used.

Some engineers may also be responsible for student interns. If this is the case, the engineer might spend part of his or her day asking the students about their research and addressing any questions or concerns the interns might have.

On another day, an engineer might conduct property research to determine who owns a piece of land the city would like to build on. A student intern might do some of the preliminary research. Once ownership of the land has been determined, the engineer must write a report to the city attorney so he or she can use that information to prepare the proper agreements and easements.

Later, the engineer might have to look over a bid or a presentation that needs to be given later that week. They may have to schedule in some time to prepare or refine the presentation. After that, they may have to explore the best construction materials for a project and then switch to a different project to review the soil and grading reports. They may need to send off CAD drawings for review or revise drawings that have been returned with feedback. At some point during the week, they will need to keep an appointment to present their bid or give their presentation.

Sometimes, civil engineers who work for the city will take calls from city residents, too. For example, if a resident is having trouble with flooding in his backyard, the city engineer will do some research and look at the original plans for the subdivision. The engineer will then go to the resident's home and inspect the property. After determining what the problem is and why the person's backyard is flooding, the engineer can make recommendations on how the problem can be fixed.

In new construction, engineers collaborate with architects. Architects are primarily concerned with the aesthetic design of a space. In a home, for example, an architect would determine where the windows and doors should be located and what size they should be, how the building should be lit, and where stairways, built-in bookcases, counters, and other design elements should go. A structural engineer's job is to understand and identify where support beams must be installed and where load-bearing walls and floors must be placed. In doing so, they

Civil engineering professors are often highly experienced engineers with a passion for educating the next generation of professionals.

ensure that the architect's vision can be realized in the most functional and reliable way possible. In the middle of a big city such as Manhattan, where a skyscraper may be involved, a structural engineer might be required to make sure any excavation and structural elements of the building do not interfere with working subway tracks located beneath the building.

Not all civil engineers work in an office or on a construction site. Some work in classrooms in colleges and universities, where they teach the fundamentals of engineering to budding professionals. Civil engineering professors must have especially strong credentials. Most are licensed PEs, have had many years of on-the-job training, and have earned a doctorate degree in civil engineering. Professors do not only teach engineering students, they also conduct research related to the civil engineering field, supervise the work of research and teaching assistants, collaborate with colleagues, and work to get their research published.

Working engineers may also attend conferences. There, the engineer can learn about new materials and methods and network with other engineers working in the same field. Conferences often involve some travel and, if the engineer plans to present at the conference, time will be required to prepare as well.

As you can see, a civil engineer's workday is rarely the same from one day to the next. As such, nearly all civil engineers work full-time. In 2012, the BLS reported that approximately a quarter of civil engineers worked overtime hours as well. Working in the private sector for an engineering or construction firm is often more demanding of your time. This is also true if you are self-employed. The trade-off is that the salary in the private sector is usually higher than what you might earn while working in a local, state, or federal government office. Civil engineers who work in the public sector may not make as much as those in private business, but they often receive better benefits and are less likely to work weekends and long hours.

While most civil engineers work in an office, some, especially construction engineers, must occasionally work in bad weather. Construction crews sometimes work in the rain, and, depending on where they are located, in the heat, the cold, and the snow. Engineers who oversee transportation projects may also have to work at night. That is the time of day least likely to impact commuters and, therefore, when actual construction takes place. Because the field is so varied, it is likely that you can find a civil engineering specialty that will suit your needs as well as your personality.

Cities of the future will rely on the innovative designs put forth by the civil engineers that are in training today.

CHAPTER 4

Into the Future

In the coming years, as the population increases and the existing infrastructure ages, the United States will need civil engineers of all specialties. Since construction projects often follow population growth, most of this demand will likely take place in urban areas. New infrastructure will be necessary for cities to grow, and older infrastructure will need to be maintained and repaired so it can continue to serve the needs of citizens. In addition, many of the experienced engineers and construction managers are expected to retire, leaving positions open for the next generation of civil engineers.

Employment Trends

A 2013 Bankrate.com study showed that getting a civil engineering degree created the third best return on investment behind advertising and economics degrees. Of the STEM fields, civil engineering is the profession with the best potential for growth. According to the BLS, civil engineering jobs are projected to grow by about 20 percent between 2012 and 2022, which translates into approximately fifty thousand new jobs. This growth rate is faster than average, compared to other occupations.

One of the largest projected growth sectors is in the area of renewable energy. For example, a civil engineer might be responsible for conducting structural analysis for large-scale solar installations. They will also be needed to **retrofit** homes and businesses with alternative energy sources. This may mean evaluating the ability of a building to support a solar array. It may also mean determining what might happen to that solar array during an earthquake or a hurricane. Engineers will also be needed to prepare sites, onshore or offshore, to support large wind turbines. Roadbeds will also need to be examined and possibly reinforced to support trucks that haul large wind turbines and other equipment.

Facilities that produce traditional power sources will also need civil engineers. Aging power plants and offshore oil rigs need to be inspected, maintained, and repaired to make sure they are safe for the people who work there, and for the environment.

In 2012, the BLS reported that about 50 percent of civil engineers worked for architectural or engineering firms. Thirteen percent worked for state government, 11 percent for local government, and 4 percent for the federal government. Those with bachelor's degrees in construction science, construction management, or civil engineering, paired with experience in the construction trade, will encounter the best opportunities.

Job prospects closely follow the general job outlook of the construction industry. Some types of construction are more sensitive to cyclical changes in the country's economy. During a recession, for example, engineers who specialize in homes, offices, and retail spaces are likely to find it more competitive to secure jobs and clients. Smaller firms or cash-strapped larger ones might lay off employees during a recession. Engineers who work for firms that specialize in institutional buildings, such as schools, hospitals, nursing homes, and correctional facilities, and heavy civil construction, such as dams and bridges, are less likely to be affected by fluctuations in the economy. However, economic downturns increase competition between established engineers and new ones, no matter what their field.

Demand is also expected to increase globally. Developing nations will require civil and structural engineers to help build infrastructure in their countries. By the middle of the twenty-first century, the United Nations projects the world's population could reach ten billion people. Engineers will also be needed to come up with viable, sustainable solutions to environmental problems and, more specifically, how these problems can be solved in the face of a growing global population.

Although more civil engineers will be needed, the BLS expects job opportunities for civil engineering technicians and drafters to stay about the same. More companies are expected to require entry-level people to hold at least a bachelor's degree, which pushes the field away from civil engineering technicians. In addition, while drafters are still expected to continue to produce technical drawings and documents, new, more efficient, software has appeared on the market. This will likely reduce the number of workers needed.

Construction processes and building technology are becoming increasingly complex. The growing sophistication in the field is leading more and more firms to require greater oversight of their projects. This requirement is driving the demand for people at the highest levels of management to have more education

How to Land Your First Engineering Job

Getting your first engineering job can be tough. One of the easiest ways is to start working for an engineering firm before you graduate. Interns often turn into full-time employees when they graduate. You will also need to take and pass the FE/EIT exam.

Networking, or seeking out and speaking to people working in the field, can be a big help as well. Some of the best ways to network include attending engineering conferences and events hosted by local science, technology, and engineering organizations. Volunteering for a charitable project, especially if you can use some of your engineering skills, is another good way to expand your network.

Remember that a career in engineering involves lifelong learning. Learning a new software program, attending an applicable seminar, or auditing additional college courses can help expand your opportunities. Be sure to add any new skills to your résumé.

Also make sure you research any company you plan to send your résumé to. Every company has their own policies, procedures, and internal culture. Learning about these things before you appear for an interview will set you apart. Finally, prepare yourself for the interview. Present yourself professionally and ask questions based on your research of the company.

and experience working with technology, environmental protection, and worker safety regulations.

Salary and Benefits

According to a 2014 Oregon State University exit survey of fifty-eight graduating civil engineering seniors, all were offered a full-time position upon graduation. Ninety-two percent accepted employment.

As of May 2012, the BLS reported that the median annual salary for all civil engineers was $79,340. The

Employee Benefits Package

Summary of Benefits

The starting salary and benefits are two of many important factors to consider when deciding between potential employers.

lowest 10 percent made less than $51,280 and the top 10 percent earned more than $122,020. The Oregon State University exit survey found that new graduates were offered between $50,000 and $60,000. The average salary for a civil engineering technician was $47,560, and a drafter earned about $49,630 annually.

Nearly all of the graduates surveyed in the poll also received benefits including health insurance, paid vacation, and an opportunity to participate in a 401(k). Some also received company stock options, a pension fund, a company vehicle, profit sharing, and/or a signing bonus.

Almost all professional, full-time engineers receive a base salary and benefits. Benefits usually include paid vacation time and sick leave, as well as health care insurance. Along with medical insurance, some companies may also offer dental, vision and eye care, life, disability, and accidental death insurance. Most also offer the opportunity to participate in a 401(k) or 403(b) program, which can help an employee save for retirement. Employees generally commit some portion of their current income to a 401(k) or 403(b) plan, and the employer matches part or all of the employee's contribution. The only difference between the two programs is that for-profit companies offer 401(k) plans and 403(b) plans are offered by tax-exempt organizations.

Getting Help and Giving Back

Professional organizations and associations provide a wide range of resources for planning and navigating an engineering career. They can help keep you up-to-date with advancements and new technologies in the field by providing periodicals, meetings, and conference opportunities. They may also offer educational courses that are needed for some types of licenses and certifications. Most associations promote the interests of their members by providing networking opportunities, which can help people find jobs or advance their careers. Some may also offer insurance or travel benefits.

Many professional engineering societies have student branches. The student associations often arrange lectures on different subjects. Getting involved in a student engineering organization is an important step. It can be especially helpful if you become active in the group by joining committees that organize speakers and seminars. Membership in professional organizations, especially if you have been a leader in the student branch of the association, should be listed on your résumé.

Another activity that can open up all sorts of opportunities, both professional and personal, is to become a volunteer. Engineers Without Borders (EWB) is an organization that brings engineered solutions to developing countries. Their members use engineering principles to help solve problems all over the world. As a member of EWB, you might help a village build a

Volunteering to work on a charitable construction crew can provide invaluable experiences.

system that provides clean drinking water to people in need, or you might help with the construction of a footbridge that links villages together. Or you might help install solar panels to light up places that are currently in the dark. The organization boasts nearly sixteen thousand professional and student volunteers who engineer solutions in over forty-five countries. Nearly all large engineering schools have a student chapter of EWB. More then 40 percent of the student volunteers are women. Volunteering in a student chapter is an excellent way to get hands-on experience before you graduate. Habitat for Humanity is another volunteer organization that you might consider working with. Where EWB can teach you engineering practices, Habitat for Humanity can help you learn the ins and outs of the construction trade.

Otherwise, they work on the same basic principles. Another way an employee's current income can be saved for retirement is to put some of their current salary into a pension plan. Pension plans are usually employer-funded, meaning that the company makes contributions to a pool of funds and invests that money on the employee's behalf. The employee then receives benefits from the pension fund upon retirement. By law, employers also pay a portion of all employees' Social Security tax, which provides retiree and disability benefits.

Some companies may offer bonuses to engineers for completing certain tasks or meeting specific milestones. Some may have profit-sharing or stock option programs as well. Still others may offer expense reimbursement for travel or cell phone charges, and possibly the use of a company car. These benefits may not seem as important as the money that appears in a monthly paycheck; however, they all increase an individual engineer's personal wealth in some way or another.

The size of the company has an enormous impact on salary and the benefits offered. There is often a trade-off between hourly salary, benefits, and opportunities for advancement, too. Larger firms tend to offer higher starting salaries and more benefits, but it may be harder to advance in the company due to more competition. A smaller company may pay less in the beginning, but rising though the ranks is easier, and with more responsibility comes a larger paycheck and sometimes more benefits.

Finding an Engineering Job

There are several career websites which can be used to find employment in the engineering and construction industry. Websites such as EngineersJobs.com are geared specifically toward engineers. This site allows you to search for open positions in specialty fields, including civil engineering, construction engineering, architectural engineering, and structural engineering. You can also search within a specific city or state. General careers site such as Monster.com or Workopolis are also good online resources.

Engineering schools and societies, like the ASCE, also provide job search assistance. The ASCE website includes a Career Connections section where individuals can search open positions and includes access to helpful resources for its members. These include résumé writing assistance, career coaching, a mentorship program, and leadership training. The organization also hosts virtual job fairs which connect prospective hires directly with potential employers.

Networking is also a highly effective tool in making connections and learning about potential job opportunities. You may want to consider creating a profile on an online professional networking site, such as LinkedIn. This is a great place to keep a list of extracurricular activities, awards, completed programs, growing skill sets, and a summary of the career you would like to have. Some young people begin building their profiles and making connections with professionals in their chosen field as early as their senior year in high school. This provides an excellent opportunity to ask questions and learn more about working an as engineer.

How to Build a Good Résumé and Prepare for an Interview

Your résumé and cover letter serve as your introduction to a hiring manager. This is the first impression they have of you. You want to make it a good one. One of the best ways to do this is to research the company and the position for which you are applying. In your cover letter, highlight any of your work experience, extracurricular activities, or college courses and seminars that directly relate to the position. Make it clear that you understand the services the company provides and the position they are trying to fill. Let them know how you can meet their needs with your skills. In your résumé, try to provide a few short sentences that highlight the engineering or problem-solving skills you have used in each of the jobs or volunteer positions you have held.

Before the interview, contact at least three people who can act as references. These people could be professors, volunteer coordinators, co-op or internship supervisors, or anyone else who can confirm that you are a skilled, responsible worker. Type up a list that includes each person's name, phone number, e-mail address, and how they know you.

When you show up for the interview, be professionally dressed and prepared to "talk shop." This means that you need to be knowledgeable about the company, so do your research beforehand. Try to find out what the company does, any notable projects they have completed, and what projects they are currently working on. Also, be prepared to talk about yourself. It might be helpful to prepare a thirty-second speech about your education, your previous work experience, what you would like to achieve in the world of civil engineering, and how these goals directly relate to the company. Also, think about your strengths and weaknesses, your accomplishments, and why you are applying for this particular position. You should also be prepared to ask questions about the company, such as what the working environment is like, what skills the best

Researching a potential employer can help you match your skills and experience to a specific job opportunity.

applicant for the position would have, and how you fit in with this vision. After the interview, be sure to follow up with a thank-you note.

The Pros and Cons of Being a Civil Engineer

Whether you find the different aspects of an engineer's job an advantage or a disadvantage is going to depend largely on your individual personality and interests. However, if the day-to-day responsibilities of one type of civil engineering do not appeal to you, perhaps another specialty will.

Working in civil engineering can be visually rewarding. As an engineer drives around their city or state, they can literally see the end result of their hard work in the roads, bridges, and other structures they have helped build. As a civil engineer, you have the opportunity to start out with an empty space and end up with a skyscraper, a bridge, or an amusement park. Alternately, you might start out with a crumbling historical monument and, through your hard work, end up with a safe masterpiece that future generations can enjoy. It is a hands-on kind of job, where you can see progress continuously and feel that something new gets accomplished every day. It can be frustrating, however, on the occasions when a project is pulled. You may spend years designing a project but, for one reason or another, the project never takes flight.

Some engineers spend a majority of their time in an office, in front of a computer. Others spend more time outdoors and on construction sites. People who work outside may love it on beautiful days, but the job may not be as pleasant on the cold and rainy ones.

Most civil engineering projects are too large for an engineer to work on alone. However, you may eventually decide to start your own engineering consulting firm. Consultants still work as a part of a team, but they often do so from home, sending technical drawings via e-mail and conducting business through conference calls and remote meeting programs.

There may be some details that a civil engineer must attend to that are not that exciting. These include reading and approving construction contracts, correspondence, permits, and reports. These tasks are often time consuming, but very important. There are also many meetings—to talk about scheduling, costs, or environmental concerns. Engineers must also address client concerns and community issues, such as construction noise, pollution, or impacts on traffic flow.

Time management is also important. An engineer cannot get so caught up in these meetings that other important issues are ignored. Sometimes meetings can be boring, but if you miss one you are not there to represent the views and concerns of the client or the workers who report to you.

Many times, a construction engineer acts as the owner's representative or, if working for the government, in the taxpayer's interests. They provide oversight to make sure everything is done correctly and on time. They may have to mediate disagreements and explain work stoppages and why the project is going over budget.

As an engineer, you may decide to work for a large engineering firm or a small one. You may work for architects or construction companies. After many years of experience, you could decide to strike out on your own and become one of the principals in your own consulting firm. You can work for a private company, a nonprofit organization, or for the local, state, or federal government. The possibilities are nearly endless.

Engineers will be desperately needed in the future. Governments and citizens are going to need them to solve problems related to the world's increasing population, energy production, and water supply. This profession provides some of the most challenging, interesting, and rewarding jobs imaginable.

However, many of today's engineers work in a fishbowl-like environment, especially those who work for the government. This atmosphere leaves them open to a lot of outside criticism—some constructive, some not. Lead engineers take responsibility for a project, which can lead to litigation. With this added responsibility, additional stress often follows. Engineers in the public sector must sell their projects publicly and politically, often to people

Innovations in Civil Engineering

Every year, the American Society of Civil Engineers recognizes one innovative civil engineering project that best demonstrates superior engineering skills and represents a significant contribution to society with the Outstanding Civil Engineering Achievement (OCEA) award. The 2015 OCEA winner was the Halley VI Antarctic research station. This state-of-the-art research facility is the first fully functional portable laboratory in the world. Its futuristic design is a result of the collaboration of the international engineering, design, and construction firm AECOM, headquartered in Reston, Virginia, and Hugh Broughton Architects of London. The $43 million project consists of eight modules, each of which sits atop four to six hydraulic legs. Each leg is individually adjustable to account for large amounts of snow and ends in an enormous ski, which allows the individual modules to be towed across the ice to different research locations. Once in place, the modules can be connected to form larger, better-equipped laboratories as well as living quarters for the scientists and engineers who work there.

Other innovative designs considered for the 2015 OCEA award included the Colton Crossing Flyover, a structure that allowed for the separation of two busy railroad corridors in California; the Echo Park Lake Rehabilitation Project, which included improving the water quality and community usage of an urban lake; the San Francisco-Oakland Bay Bridge East

Span project, the world's widest bridge and a replacement of the one that collapsed during the 1989 Loma Prieta earthquake; and the Ward County Water Supply Project, a system of wells, pipelines, and pump stations designed to bring water to parts of Texas that suffer from drought.

Engineers had to design the Halley VI research station to withstand temperatures that rarely rise above 32 degrees Fahrenheit (0 degrees Celsius) and can drop as low as −67°F (−55°C).

with no technical knowledge. In other words, engineers can no longer just design. They must be able to defend their designs, material choices, and the environmental impacts of their designs, too.

Working as a civil engineer is rarely a nine-to-five job. Since engineers often put in overtime, it is important that they are passionate about their work. Working in the public sector tends to have a little more job security than working in the private sector, where layoffs are more common. However, it never pays to take job security for granted. Any opportunity to increase your knowledge, experience, or ability to work with other people is very important. As with any job today, you have to be prepared to work hard and do the best job possible with the understanding that there are no guarantees.

Shaping the Future

If you are looking for a rewarding and challenging career in which you will rarely, if ever, be bored, civil engineering might be the right choice for you. Civil engineers will significantly shape tomorrow's built environment. In doing so, they will also have a huge influence on the direction of the country. Their ingenuity and skills will be needed to address a growing population and an aging infrastructure. They have an exciting

Professional civil engineers will help build the future.

opportunity to better each citizen's standard of living, and impact the wealth base of the nation.

The spectacular fcats of engineering and construction seen around the world today are the combined work of numerous talented people. However, many, if not more, engineers and other construction professionals are needed to shape the future. The twenty-first century is just the beginning of an exciting, creative era. Science, engineering, and technology are advancing at the fastest pace in history, and they show no signs of slowing down. The potential for innovative design and creative problem solving have never been in greater demand. In the coming decades, the skills of every nation's engineers will be needed. Are you up to the challenge?

Glossary

acoustic The properties or qualities of a room or building that determine how sound is transmitted in it.

aesthetic Design principles relating to the appearance of a structure.

alloy A mixture of two or more metals or of a metal and another element that has more desirable properties than the pure metal.

architect A professional designer who works with engineers and construction crews to bring structures into being.

blueprint A detailed, scaled technical drawing of a structure.

brace To give something added support to strengthen it.

computer-aided design (CAD) A software program that engineers use to design and refine their ideas.

constraint A limitation or restriction on a design.

corrosion The act of slowly breaking down and wearing away a material, such as metal, through a chemical reaction.

dovetail A joint formed by one or more points on one piece that interlock with corresponding notches in another.

force A push or pull applied to an object.

foundation The part of a structure beneath the ground. The foundation spreads the weight of the structure over a larger area and reduces pressure on its base.

infrastructure The basic underlying facilities and systems that allow a society to function, including transportation and communication systems, power plants, and water treatment facilities.

initiative Readiness to initiate action.

innovator Someone who develops new ideas, products, or ways of doing something.

lock An enclosed section in a canal with gates at each end used to raise or lower boats as from one level to another.

masonry A collective term for building materials made of mineral products, which includes brick, stone, cinder block, or tile.

natural resources Things found in nature that are valuable for human use, which include land, water, soil, and natural power sources, such as coal, oil, and natural gas.

retrofit To add a new component or accessory to something which was not available at the time of its original manufacture.

STEM An acronym commonly used to stand for science, technology, engineering, and mathematics.

structural member A beam which supports a structure.

technology The practical application of a body of knowledge to make new discoveries and inventions.

truss A strong frame of beams, bars, or rods that supports a roof or bridge.

Further Information

Books

Carmichael, L. E. *Amazing Feats of Civil Engineering*. Mankato, MN: Essential Library, 2014.

Silivanch, Annalise. *Rebuilding America's Infrastructure*. New York: Rosen Classroom, 2010.

Solway, Andrew. *Civil Engineering and the Science of Structures*. New York: Crabtree Publishing Co., 2012.

Websites

American Society of Civil Engineers (ASCE)
www.asce.org
A professional organization that supports, encourages, and promotes professionalism in the field of civil engineering.

Engineer Girl
www.engineergirl.com
Engineer Girl is a website designed to connect girls interested in the world of engineering with women who work in this exciting field.

Engineers Without Borders USA
www.ewb-usa.org
A volunteer organization devoted to connecting engineers with the worldwide communities that need their skills.

Bibliography

American Society of Civil Engineers. "Outstanding Civil Engineering Achievement (OCEA) Award." http://www.asce.org/templates/award-detail.aspx?id=6329.

Aragon, Greg. "A Day in the Life of a Structural Engineer." *California Construction*. http://california.construction.com/features/archive/2009/0709_F2_StructuralEngineer.asp.

Arizona State University. "Construction Engineering." http://ssebe.engineering.asu.edu/prospective-students/constengineering.html.

Bureau of Labor Statistics. "*Occupational Outlook Handbook: Civil Engineers*." Published January 8, 2014. http://www.bls.gov/ooh/architecture-and-engineering/civil-engineers.htm.

———. "*Occupational Outlook Handbook: Civil Engineering Technicians*." Published January 8, 2014. http://www.bls.gov/ooh/architecture-and-engineering/civil-engineering-technicians.htm.

Career Cornerstone Center. "Profiles of Civil Engineers: Anne J. Gorczyca, P.E." http://www.careercornerstone.org/civileng/profiles/gorczyca.htm.

National Association of Colleges and Employers. "2015 Internship & Co-op Survey." http://www.naceweb.org/uploadedFiles/Content/static-assets/downloads/executive-summary/2015-internship-co-op-survey-executive-summary.pdf.

National Science Foundation. "Science and Engineering Indicators 2014." Updated April 21, 2014. http://www.nsf.gov/statistics/seind14/content/overview/overview.pdf.

Oregon State University. "2014 Construction Engineering Management Placement Statistics." http://cce.oregonstate.edu/sites/cce.oregonstate.edu/files/pdfs/2014_cem_placement_data.pdf.

Patel, Prachi. "Engineers Without Borders." *IEEE Spectrum*. Institute of Electrical and Electronics Engineers. Published December 9, 2009. http://spectrum.ieee.org/geek-life/profiles/engineers-without-borders.

Society of Women Engineers. "Trends & Stats." http://societyofwomenengineers.swe.org/trends-stats#EEbyGender.

US Department of Transportation. "Highway History." Updated May 14, 2015. http://www.fhwa.dot.gov/interstate/faq.cfm#question1.

Weingardt, Richard. *Engineering Legends: Great American Civil Engineers*. Reston, VA: American Society of Civil Engineers, 2005.

Index

Page numbers in **boldface** are illustrations. Entries in **boldface** are glossary terms.

About the Author

Kristi Lew is the author of more than fifty science, technology, and engineering books for teachers and young readers. Fascinated with science from a young age, she studied biochemistry and genetics in college. Before she became a full-time educational science writer, she worked in genetics laboratories and taught high school science. When she's not writing, you can find her reading a book or sailing and paddling around Tampa Bay, Florida, with her husband, an engineer.